teach me patience NOW!

Equip Yourself To Be
A Business Champion

Christian Marcolli, PhD

Colin Howard Sims, PhD MRPharms

First published in Great Britain in 2010 by FocusCross Ltd

A CIP catalogue record for this book is available from the British Library.

ISBN: 978-0-9564342-0-3

Design & Typesetting by SteveClarke-ftas.com
Typeset in DIN Mittel & Minion Pro

Illustrations by Martin Bustamante, Argentina.

Printed and bound in Great Britain by Butler Tanner & Dennis Ltd.

Published by FocusCross Ltd,
2 Players Cottage, Aldenham Road, Elstree, WD6 3AQ, UK.

To my wife Sabrina for her endless support, inspiration and love, that allows me to live my dream. And to all the leaders and athletes I have worked with, for their trust, loyalty and honesty that helped me grow.

Christian

To my parents for sending me in the right direction and to Ann-Marie for reminding why. Finally, a big thank you to every colleague and friend who gave feedback and provided an environment to do so, thanks!

Colin

Contents

About the authors

Dr Christian Marcolli is the founder and owner of Marcolli Executive Excellence. He is based in Switzerland and works internationally as an executive coach, consultant, lecturer, and sport psychologist. His particular interests are the nature of leadership and the development of strategies designed to foster and achieve peak performance under difficult, changing conditions. He is as comfortable in the board room coaching corporate executives for blue-chip clients as he is positioned on the perimeter of a playing field or track coaching world-class athletes and teams. With a doctorate in Applied Psychology and his own background as a professional athlete, Christian's extensive experience as a sport psychologist for many world-class athletes allows him to evaluate the factors and strategies necessary for excellent performance under pressure for both individuals and teams.

Dr Colin Sims lives in Basel, Switzerland where he works at Vice-President level for a global company leading divisional operations via a cross-matrix team over a wide portfolio of projects. He has enjoyed a varied career working in commercial, clinical and corporate environments. Originally from Liverpool, he lived in London for over 10 years where he completed his under- and post-graduate education to become a registered pharmacist with post-graduate qualifications in clinical pharmacy and a PhD from King's College London. More recently, Colin completed an executive education program at Harvard Business School. He has lived in Switzerland for the last 10 years building and leading teams on high profile and demanding projects. He is a keen skier, cyclist and gym user, harnessing physical exertion with mental development to balance his professional and personal growth. He is widely acknowledged to have petrol rather than blood running through his veins and cars provide the focus of every other sentence.

Preface

This story began when a stressed, alpha-male, junior executive collided with a leadership consultant on a 'production line' course. The executive was in no mood to waste his time on a course he was forced to attend when felt he didn't need the feedback and was impatient for the other delegates to catch-up. His lack of interest in others on the course and the slow pace of the program quickly lead to some urgently needed feedback. Thankfully, the coach was undaunted and this was the start of a relationship which has developed into a highly successful partnership, leading both coach and executive to achieve exceptionally high levels of excellence.

Eight years later, the executive (Colin) has a Vice-President level position in a global, blue-chip company and the consultant (Chris) has established himself as a world-class leadership coach encouraging corporate executive development. Their collective experience working with executives and world-class athletes has lead them to formulate an answer to what they believe is the key question for anyone seeking excellence in what they do: What does it take to perform consistently at one's personal best in an ever changing environment? Whether the pursuit of excellence manifests as striving for a millimetre difference in a serve, or successfully leading a board of directors through a crisis meeting, Colin and Chris have identified six key components, which together make up their model of Personal Leadership Excellence – the **P⁶PROP®**. The model has been designed to help transform great corporate leaders into excellent business champions by harnessing **P**assion, **P**recision, **P**erception, **P**eace, **P**resence, **P**ersistence (**P⁶**) using the **P**ersonal **R**esource **O**ptimizing **P**erformance (**PROP**) tool.

Colin's growth from an intolerant alpha-male with an Extraversion, iNtuition, Thinking, Judgment (ENTJ) profile on the Myers Briggs Type Indicator (MBTI®), who left others hostile in his wake, to a global head of operations and successful executive spawned many adventures. Key to his success has been a series of bespoke leadership development courses for Colin and his teams. It was during one such exercise that the fundamentals of the P⁶PROP® model were identified. The rest is now in print and utilized in courses in many global organizations. Thus, this story focuses on how you too can harness personal growth to become a new generation of leader fuelled with a passion for excellence in what you do and the teams you lead!

The holistic approach of the model is critical — it not only addresses how you think but, crucially, how you behave and express those thoughts. It has been commented many times in business literature that the physical and emotional response of an executive to the challenges they face are every bit as important as the decisions they actually take… so it is time to get all dimensions of your professional and personal world aligned to embark on the discovery of excellence.

Whilst this book is a candid recollection of one person's journey seen through the eyes of the coach and the traveller, it is intended as a guidebook for everyone as the messages it promotes and behaviours it encourages are uniformly applicable regardless of the starting point. Consequently, the model does not only apply to alpha-males — it can be used by anyone who is mentally ready to undergo a voyage of personal discovery and growth. This voyage will hold many opportunities for you to learn as you pursue excellence.

CHAPTER 1

Understanding the demands
of the Corporate world

P⁶ PROP

Understanding the demands of the Corporate world

'Time is money' is a phrase all too often quoted, almost in jest, by people from every walk of life. Sadly, it is beyond true for many who laugh in public but feel the strain of trying to keep up when alone. Trying to constantly perform at your best, all day, every day, requires both skills and dedication, some of which come naturally and some of which must be learned. The **P⁶PROP®** philosophy described here has been developed to help refocus corporate executives away from today's busy schedules and on to tomorrow's performance excellence. However, this is not a book dedicated to improving your time management skills, nor a proposal for a new management approach. Although we do recognize that advances in technology and communications have lead to an exponential rise in the productivity of individuals and teams in an organization. Nevertheless, an unintended consequence of modern technology is often a loss of focus and attention on strategy and core values as we are driven towards managing our in-boxes. The relentless pressure from work 24 hours per day, seven days per week is not a sensation unique to business executives. Many individuals and teams outside of business seek to be maximally productive whilst maintaining excellence in their actions all day, every day.

Harnessing ourselves and those around us takes a combination of skills and approaches, which prior to this book have not been discussed in one place. These skills are universal, be they for parents with small children, for athletes driving themselves through another repetitive training day whilst aiming for a distant competition or for the executives described in these pages with a little distortion for comic effect.

The impact information technology has had on our working practices within one generation has been immense. It can be shocking to consider that within the timeframe of one career previously critical departments such as the typing pool no longer exist. Not because their role has been adapted and transformed into something different but because the role has been subsumed into that of the executive it once supported. The consequential change to the pace of life would not be recognizable by our parents — each day it appears as if life gets faster. Although the only thing taking longer today is a transatlantic crossing since Concorde no longer flies between London, Paris and New York: Amazingly, something a lot of executives bemoan already. So, to 'help out' every frenetic executive, airlines now have wireless and cellular telephone services on board their long-haul flights. There is truly no place left in which you can't be contacted. The last great bastion of being able to catch-up on email, sleep or both is now too consigned to the past. Those annoying ring-tones can be heard even 11 kilometers above sea level! So what's next? Are we waiting for in-flight video conferencing, which would beg the question of why are we on the plane in the first place? Does anyone ever have time to stop, to think, to reflect and to strategize on how technology, and the humans who use it, can be leveraged and should be treated? What time is left for thinking, reflecting and planning where to go, what to do and, critically, *why*?

The challenges the corporate world places today on the people who work there are huge and are no less so for the teams they interact with all day and the family members they come home to each evening or with whom they share their Blackberry's (one and only mention we promise) at the dinner table. As the pressure mounts it can manifest as lack of sleep, irritability, lack of precision and self- assurance and eventually culminate in poor performance, which in turn drives the whole cycle even harder. Everyone has their breaking point.

These factors, plus more mundane day-to-day observations made over many years drove Chris and Colin to develop the **P⁶PROP®** model for identifying and fostering the skills required for Personal Leadership Excellence. Chris is an executive coach with particular interests is the nature of leadership and Colin holds a Vice-President level position in an international corporation. The idea behind the model was to identify the key dimensions of our business life and personal perspectives (passion, precision, perception, peace, presence and persistence [**P⁶**]) and develop a structure for considering the dynamics between them **P**ersonal **R**esource **O**ptimizing **P**erformance [**PROP**]) so that we can harness our strengths whilst developing our poorer performing elements. The model is designed to help everyone improve their personal and professional life but is not a quick fix or an overnight intervention. Let us be clear, the model is a comprehensive framework that is designed for those who are ready to accept the challenge and pursue excellence. This is not for the lighthearted or the politically ambitious looking for an easy solution. You'll need to be brave, considerate, reflective and patient to develop a sustainable approach to life with excellence in everything you undertake. Most importantly, this is a journey for life and should be something to guide you in your retirement every bit as much as in your working life.

Looking forward, the world will only get more competitive and focused. Pursing excellence in everything we do, always aiming to do the right thing right, first time, every time to drive quality and consistency will have to be the standard by which we lead our lives. Excellence is not a dirty word, but a mentality influenced from within the individual and the external world in which they live and work. The pursuit of excellence beyond today's confused world is something we have to harness to be able to succeed. Although our model discusses Personal *Leadership* Excellence, we have described a platform for you to perform at your personal best, consistently and effectively over a longer period. The word 'leadership' should not misguide you into thinking about the size of your team or have you reaching for the nearest organizational chart. Leading yourself, your reports, your peers or your family should always be carried out with **passion, precision**, and **persistence** to be doing your best, along with **peace** within yourself and the **presence** and **perception** that this is not only what you want to do for yourself but what others would also expect.

So, with this as the background to **P⁶PROP®**, how can the six dimensions of our model, all conveniently beginning with the letter **P**, help you propel yourself to your highest level of personal performance? Critically, and significantly different from a number of other approaches, how can it do this in a sustainable manner and help you deliver as a business champion today and in the future?

As already highlighted, this is not an exercise for the faint hearted. Many challenging questions may be needed to help someone discover who they actually are, who they think they are and what impact they have on the world around them. For example, Professor Thomas de Long at Harvard Business School asks three key questions of each executive entering one of his programmes.[1]

How do I experience others?

Common answers include: Energetic, aggressive, draining, tedious, motivating

How do people experience me?

How honest are these answers? Amicable, competitive, concerned, confrontational, aggressive

How do people experience themselves in your presence?

What can someone else make you? Energized, activated, excited, tired, constrained, lost!

---

[1] Pers Comm. Harvard Business School, MA, USA, 10 Sept 2007 (HBS Executive Forum IV meeting)

These simple but highly direct questions can help even the hardest charging executive start down the road of self-defining pursuit of excellence. Sadly, like the stories we share with you next, insight and action are not always readily available even to the brightest, hardest working business executive. The rest of us can read and take their own perspectives on the pieces described. As you read on, whether you see yourself or not in these actions, reflect on and consider how you would have handled the situations and what you would have said to your best friend or your partner. (If you're lucky this is only one conversation, if you are like the rest of us it may take several conversations. Are men really from Venus and women from Mars? We have debated this longer than anything else in the book and concluded that we are not even that closely related to the same solar system.) This external perspective reflects a key dimension — how do others see and perceive you, professionally and privately?

So, once we have considered all these details how can we help you consistently recharge your own energy and pursue excellence on a daily basis? This question was raised by Peter Drucker[2] some years ago and we believe we have found the answer with our **P⁶PROP**® model. The central ethos is to identify and segment the controlling dimensions of our business lives, lay out a structure to handle the dynamics between them and ultimately harness our strengths whilst developing our poorer performing dimensions. Cracking this, and this is what the model is designed to do, will ensure you improve your personal and professional worlds, control your energy flow and thus increase your satisfaction with yourself, your work and your life.

---

[2]Peter F. Drucker (2001): The Essential Drucker: The Best of Sixty Years of Peter Drucker's Essential Writings on Management. New York: Harper Collins

CHAPTER 2

Passion — Are you in the right game?

Passion — Are you in the right game?

Being passionate about what you do every day is an entry ticket into playing any game at the highest level. The question is though, are you playing the same game to the same rules as those you are playing with? To develop a passion is not all that easy and finding something that ignites your passion without long periods of speculation is something to which we all aspire.

When Chris and Colin first met in May 2001 on a skills training course Colin was a hugely passionate man. In fact, Colin's passion was one of his greatest strengths as well as one of his largest potential blind-spots. "Meeting Chris was a turning point in my life, never mind my career," remembers Colin. "I had been a reasonably successful person up to that point. Professionally I always hit every goal, but sadly I didn't always notice the associated collateral damage — including a failed marriage, another failing personal relationship and not to mention a huge fixation on my work. I was defining myself through my daily outputs in the office. This was a huge personal toll to be paying, and it was being paid almost fraudulently as I lived in ignorance of how others saw me. I simply presumed that everyone else had the same level of enthusiasm for their daily tasks as I did. Moreover, that their commitment was the same unwavering 100%, all of the time and, critically, the value they placed on their work would be a non-negotiable premium.

"Sadly, it had taken the previous 12 years of positive reinforcement through excellent results to persuade me I was right. These results blinded me to the realization that the 20-hour days, 7 days per week, week in and week out was not the best way to secure excellence in my daily life. In fact, I was simply a pain to live with and working with me was not easy. Nothing was ever good enough for me and improvements could always be found. The demotivational power of that mindset on others is dramatic and destructive. Only the power of hindsight allows Chris and I to laugh together now about our first encounter because it wasn't funny at the time. Today, checking the other person is the first thing I always do, and foremost, I always ask others how much enthusiasm do you have for your work? What I am really asking is 'are you in the right game?' and if you are do you know the rules? This holds for the entire spectrum, from the super-hard charger, loud mouth, domineering, alpha wolf to the meekest and quietest colleague I work with. Beware though, the answers to this question may well shock you but must be known sooner rather than later — trying to make a tank driver into a ballerina isn't an easy task, nor one that will optimize anyone's resources. Only what really appeals to your values and your core meaning will ever deliver the passion to help you engulf life with zeal."

The reason, of course, that passion is so important is that you can only truly perform with excellence in something if you have true commitment and the drive to become one of the best in your field. You may never get there but you should always be aiming as high as you can!

"At our first meeting Colin was complaining that the pace of the course of was too slow, nothing new was being covered and he had heard it all before," Chris reflects. "This may all have been true but Colin never actually put the effort in to listen — to soak it up and take it in. I have seen this several times before, in everyone from the super shy to the excited extrovert. Listening is so different from hearing, and getting a message to stick and cause a reflection point is seldom an easy task in the hard charging world we described earlier. Yet, harnessing passion is the absolute key to personal growth and the pursuit of excellence. Feedback was quick in going Colin's direction and, surprisingly, after a night's sleep the turnaround was visible. The next morning a very worried man came to me and said, 'oh dear, what have I been doing for the last 12 years?' Actually Colin's big concern was larger than that as he had to face the course attendees for the next five days and they all perceived him as an arrogant bulldozer — not the stuff executive dreams are made of, unless of course the bulldozer is a nice brand with clear market leadership!"

The willingness to reflect and accept external perspective is a 'eureka' moment that some never get. Reflection is a crucial piece of harnessing passion but it can be easily missed through arrogance, lack of appreciation or self insight and, occasionally, sometimes just through lack of intellectual capacity to comprehend that the world is not only how you see it.

"When I met Chris," Colin adds, "I had spent the previous decade attending some of the best academic institutions in the world, training in wonderful hospitals and running successful businesses. I had a good personal life, although my ex-wife argues this point a little. I always got the results I wanted and though racked with self-doubt I always thought I was a collegiate player whose passion was visible and shared — when actually, others' perceptions were almost diametrically opposed to my own view. Chris talked slowly and purposefully with me over dinner on that first evening, describing articulately feedback based on the perspectives of others in the group. Previously, I had never once attempted to upset or trample someone and as strange as it may seem to those who have known me for a long time, this behavioural manifestation of my passion for everything I do was actually a total unknown world to me. Frankly it was quite upsetting and something I immediately adopted (with high passion of course) to set about fixing. Note to self number 1, get team together on Monday to apologize and set stage for much more feedback!"

"Colin was driven purely by ambition and perfectionism," remembers Chris. "He would always go the extra-mile to produce an even better result. As much as this inner drive was helping him to surpass many obstacles, it came to a point where he didn't have much energy left for the people around him. I do not only mean his reports, but also peers and other colleagues at work. As a consequence, there was not much empathy — he needed all his energy to perform excellently himself. All in all, Colin was not a bad guy, but he was not harnessing his passion. In fact, he became a victim of his passion. Since he was open to my feedback I explained the impact of his own energy. I was curious how Colin would respond to it."

"Shortly after this," Colin continues, "I realized that so far I had not developed a lot of passion for truly leading others. Up to this point I was very passionate and hugely committed to delivering excellent results. I looked at other people as vehicles to help me deliver, provided they didn't get in the way. I delegated, directed and generally spread things I couldn't handle in terms of volume. Reflecting now, I was a micro-manager in a very classic style, but not a leader who worked through others. With feedback from my highly supportive manager still ringing in my ears (thanks again Rajiv!), and after formalizing meetings with Chris on a regular basis, it became blatantly obvious to me that if I wanted to be successful with people I needed to change my approach as well as my mindset from 'working with people' to 'working through people'. Important to this was elevating others to a shared vision of excellence. Beyond that I needed to consider, what is excellence, how does success appear and critically how can I as a leader, coach, guide and support others to get to that stage?

"Chris and I started to speak a lot about the people I led. Not from the perspective of how good he or she was at their job, but from an understanding of their different individual and cultural backgrounds, their motives and personality patterns. This was the key for me to respect other people's approaches and build up ambition and passion to personally succeed through the successes of the team around me and my reports. This sounds simple but the critical success factors here are fundamental and careful analysis of others, clear plans and the effort to map interactions. Experiencing the positive effects of this fundamental change of mindset personally, and seeing 'my' people performing with much more enthusiasm than before, helped me realize that this was a formula for success.

"Unfortunately, I was still too quick and lacked tolerance of others who didn't want to run to keep pace with me all the time. With the amazing analytical powers that hindsight can supply, I cannot believe my lack of appreciation displayed during those times. I truly had passion but was that a passion for playing a game to my strengths? Some soul searching later I decided that I did enjoy what I do and this was the game I wanted to play."

In summary, the important point is that harnessing **passion** and applying it in a focused and measured manner is the fundamental key success factor.

P¹ PASSION

'Only passions, great passions,
can elevate the soul to great things.'

Denis Diderot (author, encyclopaedist & philosopher)

The first component of Personal Leadership Excellence
is passion. To succeed at anything requires passion,
which is present only if you are in a game that is right for
you as an individual. It is the powerhouse of creativity,
innovation and perfection as well as perseverance.
High-achieving performers are convinced they are
in the right place doing what they do best.
In the world of business this means someone who
is in just the right job, that leadership is their game
and is committed to the pursuit of continuous
personal improvement.

PASSION

Passion *is recognizing the game best suited to you and ensuring*
you have the talent to play it to the best of your ability!

CHAPTER 3

Precision — Whose rules are you following?

Precision — Whose rules are you following?

Being in the right discipline is rather obvious, as described in the previous chapter. There is no point being a pilot with a morbid fear of flying, or a skier with a hatred of the cold. Arguably, fixing your playing field to host the right game is the first thing most people do unconsciously as our passions take us in directions our brains and hearts don't always see for themselves. Now, once you are in the right game the big question is are you aware of the rules?

A great sage once said that the most powerful rules are the unwritten rules, which can apply to behaviour in society as much as family standards or work. How do you know how to behave in certain circumstances? Who told you what to do? How did you appreciate what is acceptable and what is optimal in your world? Most of the time these unwritten rules are unspoken too — how crazy is that? The values you should be playing within, the necessary rules of the game, are often things you have to learn by osmosis or passive diffusion at best. Repeated exposure to situations where the values and behaviours are displayed by actions and deeds by others seen as role models is what gives us our social and professional signposts. At home this is usually through watching and the guidance of our parents, but in the workplace the rules come through experience and observation of those who transgress the rules and are punished in one way or another — the so called game of 'politics', the most feared and hated word in corporate society, unspoken, unwritten but all encompassing.

Colin used to talk about politics and how he stayed out of them. "No need to get involved when there is a job to do, why waste your time lunching with people you can't stand?" was his favorite retort when told to be cognoscente of the political landscape in which he operated. Chris again had to help Colin, a Global Brand Manager at this stage, reposition and remarket 'politics' as 'relationships'. "Colin's skills were already developed at a high level, and together with his passion and results-orientation, he delivered strong performance almost always," comments Chris. "This was one of the reasons why he fundamentally never really needed other people's support. He would deliver anyway, regardless of external factors. However, after Colin really committed to our collaboration, he started to realize that the higher he moved up in an organization, his success would largely depend on collaborations with other people. In order to get a more positive connotation to all this I suggested we use the word 'relationships' and look at it from a more resourceful point of view.

"Now I think everyone understands relationships are important and that if you know someone it is easier to work with them, make concessions and grow as a person. Thus, Colin's next application of his passion was to focus it — or to put more simply, gain precision. This harnessing of the rules of the game, and ultimately use of them, is key to the long-term success of any business champion.

"Staying 'savvy' and keeping your eyes, ears and every other useable sense on full alert enables the rules to be learned quickly. Whether that is labeled as politics, relationships or simple working practices, behaving within the rules of the game will provide the freedom to operate at your best and therefore deliver excellence in your actions."

"I wasn't sure of the politics and thought I'd done well to avoid them," adds Colin, blissfully unaware that he was spoken about in the political maelstrom almost daily and that this was one of the biggest roadblocks to his personal growth, career and performance in the office. The first step was defining the key success factors regarding his relationships and how they manifested themselves day-to-day.

The best way to help him appreciate this environment at work was a simple exercise, via a day spent in Colin's apartment sitting at his dining table with a huge sheet paper and a lot of sticky pads. "When Chris walked in the door carrying half of the stationery cupboard I must admit my passion waned," laughs Colin. "I was not interested in the task in hand — to map out everyone I interacted with on a daily basis with respect to who they were, what they did and how they impacted on my daily work. But, by 4 pm that afternoon I had delivered (on time and on budget of course) a complete analysis of a matrix global brand team, replete with all its complexities.

"The next 30 minutes of reflection and thinking again revolutionized how I took to my work the next day. Firstly, I spent time with every single person on the chart, explaining that I was looking for two-way feedback on what mattered to them and how they saw me and those I worked with fitting into their world. The experience of the dreaded lunches and coffees was so rewarding it is now something I still do regularly with those I interact. The central growth driver was then to equip myself through training in technical skills and coaching through human or 'soft' skills to ensure that I had the tools to play the game."

"Finally, with my little world mapped out, the needs of my customers fully appreciated, the tools in hand to perform, I needed to ensure I had the right mental attitude and approach to deliver precisely what was needed. In two significant sets of activities — a feedback session on harnessing passion and being in the right game, alongside a thorough and precise analysis of the game — my professional and, dare I say, private life was starting to take a shape I could not have imagined only a few months earlier."

Chris adds, "most leaders I know look at the corporate environment and especially politics as something evil they need to deal with. Most of them try to fight it. I have advised Colin to look at it in a different, more playful way. Once he took the time to clearly identify his corporate environment he could more easily understand the relationships and therefore take an active role in effectively influencing, as well as in establishing, relationships that last longer than 'just for the job' and from which he still benefits now".

So with passion harnessed and precision set what else could there be to fix? Again, the iceberg had barely been scratched, but... being in a place where, what you don't know about what you don't know, is a warming and safe place to be. Pushing out of these comfort zones is a hallmark of someone seeking personal excellence and **passion** and **precision** is only a third of the core qualities Colin needed to explore to be able to grow.

P² PRECISION

'By concentrating on precision, one arrives at technique, but by concentrating on technique one does not arrive at precision.'

Bruno Walter (composer)

Excellent performers develop their skills until they become second nature. This ensures they can assess new situations accurately, consider alternatives and tactics depending on the situation and apply the right skills at the right time. They understand the systems and strategies around them but do not let them interfere with their performance. The skills are applied with a high level of quality and appropriate timing. The level of performance they achieve is affected by the degree of precision they achieve.

In the corporate world business champions need to have the necessary job skills to perform in a given role as well as the leadership and management skills and to be able to identify and work with changing systems and politics.

continued on page 34

P² PRECISION

continued from page 33

How fast you learn (i.e. your adaptability) is a key factor in determining how quickly you acquire precision: For example, how quickly you can adapt to a change of role, function, level or even a job, which in today's corporate world can happen at very short notice. Although this is an influencing factor in the learning process, it is viewed as a stable factor of an individual's personality and, therefore, is not discussed further.

PASSION **PRECISION**

Precision *is identifying and following the rules to ensure daily excellence in your game*

CHAPTER 4

Perception — Do you trust yourself and others?

Perception — Do you trust yourself and others?

"Amazingly, my then partner wasn't scared by the rapid changes to Dr Listen," Colin jokes. He had been busy focusing his game and getting himself technically armed with player status. Then, another key success factor he hadn't appreciated properly loomed in front of him and the need for a safe, stable and trustworthy private environment reared its head as a crucial place to explore and share his new skills.

"Colin never really looked at his private relationships as a resource for his performance at work," explains Chris. "In fact, it seemed to me that he was not open to any feedback from his private environment about his professional world. On the one side, I think it is absolutely necessary that there is a separate world out there which allows us to ground ourselves on another level. On the other side, in the high-paced performance world Colin inhabits it is important to try to integrate both worlds, and I believe is one of the cornerstones of work-lifestyle-integration."

"I remember my other half saying that I would come in from the office (late of course) and then need to be left alone to either cook, stare at the fire or do something alone for the first 30 to 60 minutes of getting home," acknowledges Colin. "This was always at odds with my hugely extrovert personality, but was time I seemed to need to just get my day out of my system and calm down. This behaviour was actually quite alienating to those closest to me (so much so that despite many years together we finally decided enough was enough and parted company) as she wanted to know what had happened in my day, share what had happened in hers and provide comment or help and contribute to solving my problems. This is something I now value hugely in my new partner and something I should have recognized a long time ago. It takes a very special person to be strong enough to give articulate feedback, be intelligent and sensitive yet share their professional day too. This is something we have arrived at only after lots of communication developed during a couple of years in a long-distance relationship, which hones such skills. Although we now live in the same place we both travel internationally and as such have to continue working on the communication whilst we are both in a variety of stressful business situations all over the world. My only comment is to always treat your partner better than your friends. As stupid as this appears on paper, it is so often that those closest are taken for granted and not appreciated at all! Never break this rule. The stability and external strength afforded by a strong personal relationship is one of the critical success factors I have discovered on my journey and is pivotal to significant achievements."

People handle stress in many different ways. What Chris has observed in his varied experience dealing with world class athletes and sports people, as well as corporate executives, is that if they can not perceive themselves as being in a solid, and more importantly safe, environment in both their personal and professional lives the imbalances can quickly pile up if things are not shared or reflected on with others. Moreover, the input or external reflection and de-contextualization is a critical way of ensuring that your passion and precision are all going in the right direction and are aligned with both your personal and professional goals (more of this later).

Transparency at work has been a hallmark of Colin's professional life, but again ensuring the context and balance of this transparency is a further success factor often under appreciated. "Having the ability to share openly with professional colleagues really has opened up a quality in thinking and planning I had not previously seen despite numerous successes," adds Colin. "A non-threatening learning environment is a real plus to any relationship, again whether private or work based. In fact, even today, in 2009, the open learning style is one we use every minute at my current company. Empowered and self-learning people have produced some truly inspirational ideas and deliverables. I never underestimate how crucial it is to create that trusting and stable environment and its contribution to success."

"In addition, the fact that there are a couple of people I fully trust (at work and in private), has in return provided me with an extra resource of candid feedback. It took a while to establish these relationships, although Chris told me right from the start that if I wanted a stable environment I would need to show my vulnerabilities.

This was not easy for me. Being vulnerable with people, even the closest ones, made me feel extremely uncomfortable, like I was giving away some sort of control over the environment. Nowadays, I still very much focus on controlling whatever I can, but I have become much more relaxed and open to the people I know will support me no matter what."

With growing **passion** and **precision** and the **perception** of trust and stability we are half-way through the core dimensions that make up Personal Leadership Excellence. Although crossing these bridges with reports, peers, managers, partners, and family are time consuming and take dedication the rewards for doing so are multifold.

P³ PERCEPTION

'People only see
what they are prepared to see.'

Ralph Waldo Emerson (essayist, philosopher, poet)

Perception in this context describes the ability to understand the external environment or, more practically, the ability to identify which people you can trust (at work and in private). Being able to depend on a small number of people for emotional and social support is crucial for high performers.

A safe environment for sharing inner thoughts and feelings develops emotional belonging and bonding.
These relationships also provide honest and open feedback about how you are perceived, which in turn, helps you to grow continuously. This, ultimately, allows you to develop the ability to trust and let go.

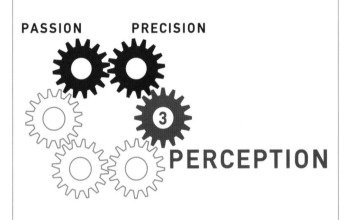

PASSION   PRECISION

3

PERCEPTION

Perception *is building the secure environment —*
the ability to identify which people you can trust fully
(at work and in private)

CHAPTER 5

Peace — Are you settled within yourself?

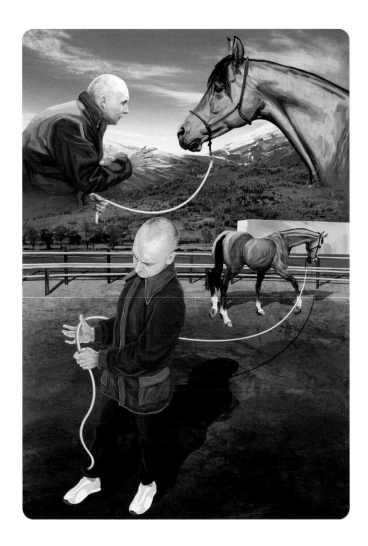

Peace — Are you settled within yourself?

Colin's partner in the days before the coaching began decided that her life living with a fire-gazing sociopath wasn't the way forward and somewhere between the door and the car park declared that if he ever wrote an autobiography it should be called "Teach me patience — NOW!". As you can see we took this to heart and is the next big dimension for knowing yourself and defining your future, alongside a detailed appreciation of the path you took to where you are today.

"I must admit that whenever someone said 'I'm off to Nepal to find myself', I was never quite sure what irritated me most," muses Colin, "the finding themselves bit, the need to do it somewhere perceived as exotic and environmentally damaging (the man-made mess and lack of weekly trash collection is staggering in the foothills of the Himalayas) or the fact that Nepal was a little difficult for the average secondary school student to pinpoint on a map.

"Thus, the next significant cliff I fell over, blindfold and ignorant, was the one where appreciating what makes you who you are is critical to your personal growth. Funnily enough when Chris and I had sat down to audit what good habits would look like, what I do today and what I have done in the past, it became pretty simple to find myself in the non-jet lag inducing space of my living room."

"As I had built a clear picture of the game that suited me best and the rules I needed to follow to play it, plus an appreciation of my external environment, the obvious gap was an understanding of what makes me, me. These truly deep and thought-provoking issues came out loud and clear from a detailed 360-degree feedback session I had taken part in as part of my personal development plan at work. Layered over how others saw my strengths and weaknesses, I had a chance to clarify for the first time on paper how I saw myself. This was a really soul searching exercise and needed a very long day, but with a clear deliverable — a bit like the people map from the earlier chapter. I needed a detailed audit of what I felt I did well, what I felt I didn't do well and what I aspired to be as a person.

The shock of the difference between how I saw myself and how Chris and others (via an 18-person 360-degree feedback exercise) saw me was a little bit like base jumping without the parachute. For every vote I gave myself for being a thought-provoking catalyst, I was seen as a 'my way or the highway' bully — the exact opposite of what I was trying to achieve. So, what came out of the feedback exercise, a day locked in a room with a blank sheet of paper and a set of instructions was one clear point — I was not at peace with myself or self-aware enough to leverage the skills I had already gained over the years. Chris pointed out that perhaps it wasn't what I was thinking or saying but how I was expressing it externally that was causing me a problem. His next inspired idea, which I immediately thought was as useful as an economy trip to Nepal, was a session at a farm in Chur in eastern Switzerland. Given the successes of the previous coaching sessions my reluctance to go was quickly overcome and one cold December morning we set off.

"Cold became the key descriptor of the day. At a fruit farm in the shadow of the snow-covered Alps was a horse ménage and the Swiss equivalent of a horse whisperer (not quite Robert Redford and certainly no sign of Kristen Scott

Thomas). As a man who grew up in major cities and had never been near a horse before I was prepared to remain open minded for a few minutes (see I was already more patient than earlier). Horses apparently have the mental age of a 3-year old child. They only understand what to do from clear directions and instructions. Plus, this was Switzerland and the horse could not understand English so non-verbal communication was the lesson of the day. The old saying 'actions speak louder than words' was where Chris was taking me, trying to get me to understand that when crisis looms the physical behaviours and emotions shown through those behaviours communicate every bit as loudly as what is said and written.

Anyway back to the horses, a cold field and snow-covered Alps. I entered the ménage and under close instruction spent a whole day making a horse go backwards, sideways, kneel down, trot in circles and generally do my bidding. All of which was achieved with no previous experience, just with the use of clear actions and expectations to make something happen. This may seem disconnected from finding yourself and establishing who you really are, but when you realize that your every action induces a reaction in those around you, you rapidly learn that your actions need to be controlled more tightly than anything else you do.

Laughing today looking back at this activity some 6 years ago, Chris realizes that whilst the activity was a leadership exercise, the day with the horses actually held a huge mirror up to Colin to help him see exactly what his actions do to undermine the content of his thinking. "When I met Colin I listened and could hear genuine concern and thinking going on," notes Chris, "but I was quickly exhausted by the fast pace at which ideas came and the lack of clarity this speed brought about. Plus, his sarcasm and wit could distort the message for those who don't have English as their mother tongue. Or even if you do understand the jokes, having some time to listen effectively is always a key dimension of effective communication. Thus, I tried to help Colin find his own inner peace through a self-learning exercise of how he comes across. This sort of exercise can be used to help anyone from the most introverted person to develop a presence, to the world's greatest showman be clear how he wishes to interact with those who matter around him."

Turning these new observations into something tangible and then practicing them was a major driver now for Colin's developmental path. Defining the good habits he wanted to display and then pulling together a plan to ensure that the habits were maintained was key.

"After thawing out from the day with the horses in the icy winds of Chur I arranged another protected office day with Colin," remembers Chris. "Colin's ability to clear his diary and 'take time to make time' was already a reflection of the personal growth he was undertaking, but more importantly, this was the day we sat and defined what good habits look like and a number of realizations were made. A significant discovery was that the daily exercise period should be used as protected time to reflect, not to work or make phone calls related to work. I remember giving Colin a cartoon which he still has on his office wall today. It has two pictures of a man sitting on a river bank fishing. In one picture the man is relaxing and watching his fishing rod, in the other the man is typing away furiously on his laptop. I wrote over the top 'remember you grow when you rest'. This has become a hallmark of Colin's voyage over these years. His extreme sense of action had prevented him from reflecting, but as part of his daily exercise routine he could now take time to think and could build this into his pattern of good habits he wanted to follow for the future.

"Colin went through the usual programs teaching priorization and time-management. Although he was very effective in applying these principles, he realized quickly that he would never be done, no matter how well he prioritized. The workload was simply too big to ever be completed. This fact caused Colin a lot of stress and he fought it for a long period of time thinking that he just needed to do more in less time and it would finally end up as a well-defined, manageable working day."

Soon after the start of their collaboration, Chris shared a fundamentally different perspective with Colin. In the fast-paced world of today it is not about managing time, but about managing energy. It is about the ability to recover and rejuvenate on a regular basis in order to be fresh and agile under the premise that you will never be finished anyway. "It never got so clear to me as in that moment," said Colin.

"Under this premise, we started to analyze Colin's resources for energy, much more than his distribution of time," continued Chris. "Colin realized that he needed to take care of his physical energy to stay fit in this highly stressful environment, and that he had to be careful with his emotional energy as well."

Most important though was the energy from his core values, which Chris and Colin analyzed together in what they called 'his story': How was his upbringing? What were the implicit and explicit expectations of him when he was a child? What kind of patterns did he take from this into his current world?"

"For this, Colin was asked to be a researcher of his story in a particular way," notes Chris. "He was asked to look back and reconstruct the essence of his life in a very structured way, bringing photographs from different stages of his life, analyzing the histories of his father and mother, bringing maps from the different places he has lived, collecting things that have a meaning for him so that he carries them with him when he moves and putting together a collection of the music he listened to in the different years. On one day, Colin laid everything out in my office and we started to go through Colin's story like a movie with the goal of developing a clear and conscious understanding of where Colin comes from and where his roots are. Based on this, we could have a discussion about what his core values are using what he has experienced in life so far."

As Chris points out, "This is a very powerful process that I apply with many high performers. They often underestimate the influence of their upbringing and don't understand, for example, their need for perfectionism from which most high achievers suffer. By having a crystal clear understanding of their story so far, we can usually identify the root causes. This is the only way to get inner peace — you need to understand who you are and where you come from, what is functional and what is dysfunctional — in order to be able to let go, and sometimes also forgive. I then even go one step further. It is not only about accepting, but appreciating your uniqueness by being clear about your values combined with your unique story."

Colin identified the following values: authenticity, honesty and loyalty, as well as a sense of equity and fair-play. This was the core outcome for him from this exercise and provided him with something deeper he could go back to every time he is faced with a major decision in his career and life.

"In many cases, you cannot plan a career in every detail," Chris adds. "A career often just 'happens'. During the evolution of a career, however, you will be faced with many decisions you need to make. If you are aware of your passion, you know what you are good at, you have people who you fully trust and you know your core values you will most probably make the right decision and somehow be positively surprised how well you progress. To me, this is the key to advancement, in any professional field. The goal is to write your own unique story and be excited about it — you have to be smiling when you think about your own life."

Thus, as Colin's voyage of personal growth continued we had orientated him in his external environment by harnessing his **passion**, honing his **precision** and ensuring his **perception** of the environment was solid. We can now start to provide some balance to this heavy external view with the **peace** component developed from personal awareness and an appreciation of his own history.

P⁴ PEACE

'When a man finds no peace
within himself it is useless
to seek it elsewhere.'

LA Rouchefoliocauld (author)

Inner peace is the process of being in harmony
with yourself and your perspective on life and requires
a high degree of self-awareness and self-acceptance.
Knowing and accepting yourself allows you to be grounded
within yourself, to remain confident and to develop optimal
behaviours of personal effectiveness.
To achieve this you must know your own strengths and
weaknesses as well as your personal preferences in order to
recognize your 'good habits' for sourcing and managing
your energy (physical, emotional and mental). You will then
know how to stay in control of your impulses by
developing alternative responses for situations you
don't normally encounter.

In order to reach inner peace, it is important that you have a vision of where you want to go and what you want to achieve built on your own understanding and appreciation of your personal history.

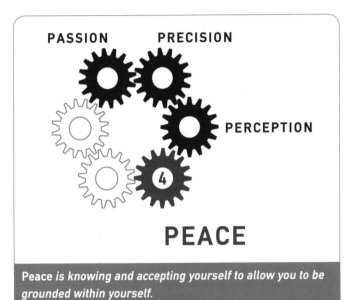

PASSION   PRECISION

PERCEPTION

PEACE

Peace *is knowing and accepting yourself to allow you to be grounded within yourself.*

CHAPTER 6

Presence — Are you authentic?

Presence — Are you authentic?

Similar to non-verbal, and to some extent verbal, cues described in the previous chapter how you harness your peace and then externalize it through communication is a key dimension. People who behave against their core peace generate a lot of stress for themselves. This so called 'behaving against type' described by most Jungian-based psychologists is possible for anyone to do and most of us do so most days, at least for a small part of our day. Indeed, a lot of people can behave against type and feel no stress at all in their daily lives, how many friends do you know who complain about their job almost every day of their working lives? And for some well into their retirement! But, the key question is whether behaving against type, or not being authentic to yourself, is sustainable over time? Even more pertinent, is whether you want to live your life being something you are not?

With a lot of business champions, who understand their game all too well, losing authenticity is something they feel they have to do to fit in. Here is where the authors of this book disagree with this perception. Chris has worked with some of the world's leading athletes and Colin has worked in a diverse range of successful, internationally recognized companies. However, neither has ever felt the need to compromise who or what they are to live their life. In fact, when any compromise on this point has been made the stress and anxiety felt was highly destructive.

Thus the recommendation is to be authentic. Having presence in your private and professional life will help you perform with excellence no matter what you do.

Being authentic, however, is not just being 'one way' all the time. "When I work with my clients, I spend quite a lot of time to find out who they really are by focusing on their own story of their life so far," comments Chris. "After this, I look at their *persona* from two different angles. Who are they in private, what characteristics make them unique in their personal environment? I then review the characteristics regarding their professional life. Who are they as a performer and what makes them distinctive? Both facets of their *persona* are important. It is absolutely necessary to understand and clearly distinguish between 'your' characteristics at home and at work."

A seminal dimension of performance in the sphere of excellence is how you connect and engage with people and handle yourself and others in various situations that arise. The core exercises Colin and Chris engaged in were actually some of the least structured parts of the coaching road they followed. Chris actually accompanied Colin in his daily working life over a number of events. This helped Chris to give focused, example-driven feedback in 'real time' as well as providing him with an appreciation of how matrix global teams function in high-pressure environments. This exercise really underlines that no matter what stress or pressure you operate under it is crucial to remain authentic, focused and well orientated. In fact, the ability to express yourself honestly is a crucial skill that allows you to be authentic.

"One of Colin's strengths has always been his compelling communication-style," notes Chris. "It helped him a lot to catch other people's attention and to have an energetic impact on others. Combining this with good eye-contact, Colin makes a natural impact on others. I pointed out this strength to him and encouraged him to communicate this way as much as possible, not to try to be tactical or say what others may want to hear."

On one such 'immersion' trip in 2003 Chris accompanied Colin to a major healthcare business congress in Berlin. For a lot of delegates congresses are a mixture of learning, dining and socializing, which generally provides a good balance of benefits. However, if you are a sponsor of the event and leading a team that has to deliver to demanding internal and external audiences the picture is significantly different.

"So you can imagine my surprise," says Chris, "when Colin was up before me every morning for our 'run in the sun' as he called it. This was no small jog, but a solid hour running around the Tiergarten and up through the park and under the Brandenburg Gate. After the run, a few stretches in the park and a shower Colin then immersed himself into almost 18 hours of solid meetings, lectures and contacts with people. This time pressure and intensity for over a week certainly had me, as a former professional athlete, impressed by how the corporate world places similar challenges on its people to the sports world. Through the whole exercise I watched Colin drive himself daily to be authentic and genuine in his every interaction and frankly I can't imagine people being able to handle demanding situations like this if they are not sure of themselves and their purpose. This helped me realize that the view others have of an individual must be balanced with the individual's internal perspective. The Berlin trip proved a turning point for the coaching between us. The start of each day, complete with morning workout, really helped the 'take time to make time' planning approach, which is a hallmark of excellence in leadership. The daily run provided time to deconstruct the key learning points from the previous day and generated a clear roadmap and description of what success would look like for the day ahead and helped to keep us focused on specific and important events rather than feel overwhelmed by the volume of work. This approach, plus learning from the past to prepare for the future, is a daily vignette on how we viewed Colin's career thus far: Take stock, define success at the highest level, plan how to get there and do not waver from the path unless course-altering factors prevail. This is a recipe for delivering excellence in execution and as exciting as the trip to Nepal would have been, an intense week in Berlin worked well. But, joking aside, any work situation can act in the same way and help any coach guide their mentee to new levels through hands on experience and not through contrived situations alone.

"One of the things I really appreciated with Colin, right from the start when we first met, was his authenticity. I never had the feeling he wanted to pretend to be somebody else, and I got this feedback also from other people. 'With Colin you know what you get' was a familiar refrain. When he was on his game he had a fantastic ability to connect with people. On top of that, he already had an excellent way of expressing himself. Putting all this together, Colin was an authentic person living under the premise 'like me or hate me, I don't care'.

"Generally, knowing that you cannot be liked by everybody is not a bad attitude, but there is a point when it can become too much. At times Colin was too authentic — saying things that would have been better kept to himself, unaware of the impact of his bluntness. This is why I asked him undertake the process of self-awareness first, described in the previous chapter, so that he could distinguish between being natural or authentic and bluntness. We put the work under the motto 'Be authentic but don't be stupid about it!'"

In summary, the path to personal excellence has to be a balance between external perceptions and internal emotions and thinking. Externalizing oneself through **passion**, **precision** and **perception** whilst balancing **peace** and **presence** (as described in this chapter) provide a solid foundation and define whether you are an authentic leader. This chapter has told a story of someone who is highly authentic having the courage to be so in a sustainable way.

P⁵ PRESENCE

'You can't talk your way out of something you behaved your way into. You have to behave your way out.'

Doug Conant (CEO, Campbell Soup Company)

One of the most admired characteristics of any leader or performer is presence. They have poise and authority and the confidence to be authentic as well as the courage to be unique and do things in their own way, highlighting their passion and demonstrating how it can be harnessed. The ability to express themselves clearly and concisely are essential characteristics of someone with presence and charisma. Effective leaders can engage and connect with people honestly, and instinctively.

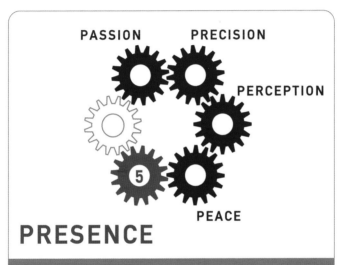

PASSION PRECISION PERCEPTION PEACE

PRESENCE

Presence *is being fully aware of your roles and being authentic to yourself and others day in, day out.*

CHAPTER 7

Persistence — Are you self-disciplined?

P⁶ PERSISTENCE

Persistence — Are you self-disciplined?

Who would admit they lack discipline with their good habits? After all everyone cleans their teeth three times a day don't they? As silly as this may sound, your habits as a leader and someone who is seeking excellence for themselves as a business champion must have a set of good habits, which you adhere to as strongly as the routine of cleaning your teeth. Persistence in whatever you do is the final chapter in the pursuit of excellence. Based on the discussions in earlier chapters it is easy to see how specific habits can be defined to address both external and internal dimensions of the essence. The external focus is how you build and maintain relationships and the internal focus is how you build and maintain yourself as a person.

Cultivating high-quality relationships is the foundation many need to progress from mediocrity to excellence by relying on the external perspective of others. Thus, the quality of the dialogue and relationships you have with others will be directly proportional to the quality of Personal Leadership Excellence you ultimately deliver. Discipline is a strong word but one which describes the habits of those seeking excellence — when was the last time you heard the world's best sportsman or woman had rolled over at their 5 am alarm call and said 'I can't be bothered this morning, I'll train the night before I play!' Our point precisely. A lot of parallels can be drawn between the preparation of athletes and business champions. Tenacity, power, aptitude, talent and natural skills are great and a must to succeed but, crucially, the discipline to apply these abilities and continue with training is what always singles out the great from the good.

This brings us to Colin's Achilles heel in the balancing act between the dimensions discussed so far. "Colin had no patience — absolutely none whatsoever," smiles Chris. "Some years ago, he would lose his patience often instead of controlling his impulses. Even today, years after becoming great friends, I still see Colin have to bite his tongue and control himself when his patience evaporates milliseconds after something irritates him. Can you imagine the level of stress this must cause him internally? I felt I had to do something, so I devised a plan for a day out to demonstrate the benefits of patience.

I asked Colin to pick me up early on an amazingly beautiful August morning but refused to tell him where we were going. I only gave him the next direction when he needed it. This was driving him mad but he was already seeing the point that he didn't *need* to know where we were going, he just *wanted* to know. This is a big difference and was something our day was designed to impress upon him.

"So how do you torture someone with no tolerance or ability to sit still for more than a second? By making them do something that takes a lot of time and patience." Chris gleefully points out…

So the final piece in the puzzle of defining personal excellence took Chris and Colin, who had fully embraced the idea of growing and changing for the better, to the top of a hill. Both were amazed by the views from the top on this perfect summer morning overlooking the Vierwaldstättersee in the heart of Switzerland.

"So there we were," says Chris, "sitting over-looking the lake on a beautiful summer's day with a stunning view of the Alps and Mount Pilatus. Not the most taxing way to spend your day. But, all Colin could see was the task before us and that time was ticking. I had taken along a huge pile of broken tiles and the task was to make a mosaic to take home. We spent the day just talking, gluing and grouting our mosaics together. Colin saw the point from the first second but it took him hours to relax into it, appreciate what he was doing and his surroundings. Now it may sound a little extreme and the objective here was not to complete the mosaic (which became a side table and still takes pride of place in his living room). The learning was that sometimes great things take time, and developing that self control to take a deep breath and relax to enjoy a view or a moment is what makes life rich and rewarding.

"The pace Colin was on had great potential for burnout. It was just amazing how many hours a day he put into his work, and even when he was not at work, he was attached to his mobile devices or laptop. Once he understood that it was his energy he needed to manage carefully, not his time, it became clear to him that persistence in the way he was applying his good habits was the key for long-term success" reminisces Chris.

"Before becoming physically fit, Colin had a tendency to compensate for his lack of exercise with emotional highlights — such as nice dinners with good wine. He realized it didn't do him any good in the long-term, but he felt that he deserved it after a very busy day at work. He was satisfied in the short-term, but frustrated in the long-term. It was very clear to me that Colin could only transform the amount of stress he experienced if he was physically in shape. Many leaders and executives underestimate the correlation between physical fitness and the ability to manage stress and pressure effectively. For many years Colin didn't exercise as he didn't think it had much to do with his ability to perform his job. However, after a discussion, and reviewing a couple of research studies, he was convinced we needed to integrate a training program into his working life.

I do not want to turn my clients into athletes, but regular exercise makes them feel strong and is an absolute must."

This is a cornerstone of Chris' thinking and one never for negotiation.

The best athletes in the world have developed routines to maintain and protect their energy under pressure, and this is the concept behind an exercise programme for executives too. Once the disciplined training programme became a habit Colin started to feel the benefits. In order to save time (going to the gym was not an option given the workload), he bought himself a cross-trainer and got up every morning an hour earlier than usual to work out. Slowly, as he became fitter, the exercise programme increased and he became very conscious about his nutrition. This combination resulted in losing a couple of kilos in only a few weeks, but more importantly, he had a much better feeling about himself and became physically stronger to transform the pressure into something productive.

So finally Colin had assessed the three major external factors **passion**, **precision** and **perception** and balanced these with the three internal dimensions of life **peace**,

presence and **persistence**. Did he learn *patience*? Well that would be telling, but Colin has leveraged these six dimensions in a balanced and consistent way to a achieve a senior, strategic, leadership-level position in a company which prides itself on a performance culture with a clear set of values and behaviours. Colin's personality has led to many amusing observations, some of which are shared here, but whether you follow the same personality traits or have your own unique profile there is a framework here for individuals to grow in a structured and proven way and drive themselves to perform consistently at a level of excellence, which is complimentary to who they are and how they live their professional and personal lives.

P⁶ PERSISTENCE

'We are what we repeatedly do.
Excellence, therefore, is not
an act but a habit"

Aristotle (philosopher)

The final component of the P⁶PROP© model is persistence.
The most impressive trait of any world-class performer
is their unremitting effort to produce personal-best
performances over and over again. In the long-term,
this level of peak performance can be exhausting.
They only become champions by establishing good training
habits — tailor-made routines and rituals designed for
maintaining their bodies and environment in optimum condition.
They also pay particular attention to the balance between
performance and recuperation, which means they are able
to switch off from training on a regular basis.
Taken together, high-level performers establish
routines that provide emotional stability
allowing them to perform consistently alongside
the space to recharge their energy.

Excellent performers call on this emotional stability
when they experience failure (you cannot always be
a champion, but you can always behave like one)
and they are able to resist the temptations of success,
such as a sense of complacency.

Persistence *is having the self discipline to be at your best each and
every day in every activity.*

CHAPTER 8

Using the
P⁶PROP® model

Using the
P⁶PROP® model

In business the term 'excellence' has been used for many years in many different contexts. Almost every publication on business excellence focuses on two questions:

— *What enables you to become great*
at what you do?

— *What allows you to perform at the*
highest levels of excellence?

While there is no doubt that discussions about high performance must include these two characteristics, we believe the concept of excellence should be viewed more broadly reflecting the whole person:

— *What does it take to harness your*
full potential?

— *What does it take to perform at your*
personal best consistently over years
regardless of changes to your
environment and circumstances?

The **P⁶PROP**® model of Personal Leadership Excellence directly links the concept of excellence to an individual's potential for high performance. This leads to a more holistic understanding by harnessing potential as fully and consistently as possible. This is the only way to become a great business champion and stay at the top. In other words, even though situations and environments change constantly, excellent performers become and remain great as a direct consequence of their passion for, and pursuit of, excellence. This passion and ongoing quest differentiates the business champion of today from the corporate leader of yesterday.

The dimensions of the engine we have described, through our hopefully humorous examples, in previous chapters culminate in a powerful, fully integrated engine which taken as a whole can be harnessed to drive the propeller, which can either push you to levels of excellence you never previously envisaged or pull you back, dragging on your aspirations. From here it is time to start to harness the thrust the propeller can give you when applied to the right engine and orientated in the right way

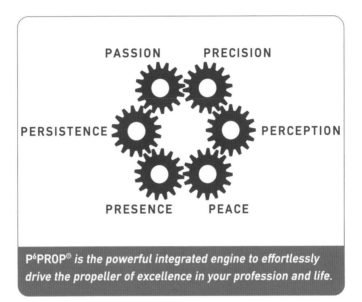

PASSION   PRECISION

PERSISTENCE   PERCEPTION

PRESENCE   PEACE

P⁶PROP® is the powerful integrated engine to effortlessly drive the propeller of excellence in your profession and life.

Why do business champions have to display excellence?

The corporate world has become an arena that demands the same high performance standards seen in world-class athletes and this will only intensify in the future. The parallels between these two worlds are evident despite the diversity of individual differences and personality traits or whether the athletes are training for individual or team sports. The building blocks of excellence are the same and once they are understood, and the way they interact, it becomes easy to assess whether someone is capable of excellence or not.

Your own success as a business leader can be defined by your pursuit of personal excellence. Similar to world-class athletes, business champions have to perform consistently when exposed to heavy competition (within and outside their organization), manage an immense workload and stay calm and focused under pressure. Pressure will come from many places: new corporate structures with complex operating environments; leaner teams; enhanced information technology driving an increase in the speed and volume of business; budget constraints and constant requests for faster delivery and higher quality. Business champions are also expected to deliver outstanding personal and team performance. To do this consistently and reliably requires more than the luck of 'a favourable phase' or 'everything just coming together right now' — it requires Personal Leadership Excellence. The mental attitude central to building a successful professional career requires determination to get the best out of yourself, your team, and the situation. Peak performance will deliver the predictability, control and consistency necessary for success.

Defining the P⁶PROP® model of Personal Leadership Excellence

The **P⁶PROP®** model of Personal Leadership Excellence provides a framework for individuals to gain a better understanding of themselves, the business environment in which they work and the skills they need to be consistently successful. Once these skills are mastered, the rewards can be immense in terms of job satisfaction, monetary recompense and professional development. The earlier in a career this is applied, the higher the chances that a business champion will make it to the top and stay there.

PROP stands for **P**ersonal **R**esource **O**ptimizing **P**erformance and the **P⁶PROP®** can best be visualized as six propellers, the six blades of a propeller being driven by a fully integrated, harmonious engine behind it – each blade of the propeller corresponds to a '**P**' component described in the earlier chapters as P^1 to P^6. The thrust achieved by the propeller is determined by how well each component, or blade, performs and the maximum thrust is achieved when all blades work together efficiently to deliver optimum power. A score can be given to each propeller blade to describe how well the component is contributing to the performance of the engine: positive, neutral or negative impact. The components of the $P^6PROP^®$ model are interrelated and thus the scores for P^1 through to P^6 are the key to understanding the overall $P^6PROP^®$ score and the business champion's overall potential for excellent performance.

Harnessing excellence

The ultimate behavioural consequence of the $P^6PROP^®$ model is Personal Leadership Excellence. This means that a business champion is passionate about what they do, has the necessary skills to perform at a high and effective level, works within an environment that allows them to perform and grow, leverages inner peace through being in harmony with themselves, has a strong authentic presence and is able to reproduce peak performance on a regular basis because they are persistent in recuperating their energy. Figure 1 shows the optimal scores of one individual using the **P⁶PROP**® model. The results illustrate that the individual has developed all six **P**-components to such a high degree so that no additional energy is required to be at their personal best. As a consequence, the individual will experience the maximum amount of thrust when performing.

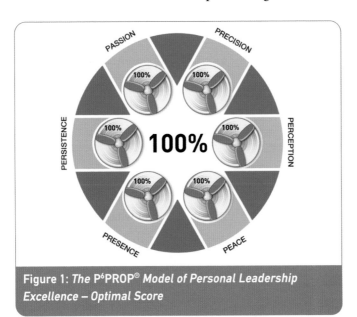

Figure 1: *The P⁶PROP® Model of Personal Leadership Excellence – Optimal Score*

How you can apply the P⁶PROP® model to achieve Personal Leadership Excellence

First, you need to diagnose your current level of Personal Leadership Excellence. You can do this with introspection, reflection and feedback from people with whom you live and work closely. The six fundamental questions you need to review provide the basis of the **P⁶PROP®** model and are summarized below. Based on the assessment received you can identify the areas that are limiting your ability to achieve Personal Leadership Excellence and devise a programme to help you address any problems and capitalize on the successful components.

Passion (P¹) — *Are you in the right game?*

How much enthusiasm and adour do you have for your work? Does it have deeper value and meaning for you? How much commitment have you developed to become one of the best in your field?

Precision (P^2) — *Have you mastered the techniques of the game?*

Do you have accurate understanding of the success factors in your role? Have you have acquired the skills to succeed? Do you have an excellent knowledge of the systems and politics? Do you have the mental skills for success in your role?

Perception (P^3) — *Do you have a stable environment that you fully trust?*

Do you have a safe, stable and trustworthy private environment? Do you have a safe, stable and trustworthy business environment? Do you have an excellent relationship with your manager?

Peace (P^4) — *Do you know yourself inside and out and appreciate your uniqueness?*

Do you have an excellent understanding of your personal history and vision of the future? Do you have crystal-clear self-awareness? Do you know your 'good habits'?

Presence (P^5) — *Are you authentic?*

Are you fully aware of your role(s)? Are you truly authentic in your interactions? Do you efficiently connect and engage with people and situations? Do you articulate and express yourself well?

Persistence (P^6) — *Are you disciplined with 'good habits'?*

Do you apply your 'good habits' consistently? Do you cultivate high-quality relationships, especially in periods of stress? Are you disciplined with your 'good habits' — have you ritualized them?

The P⁶PROP® Inventory

The **P⁶PROP®** Inventory is a questionnaire, which is completed by the individual being profiled, people close to the person at work (i.e. a peer, direct report or manager) and a person in a position of trust outside work. For each of the six components, there is a series of questions which are answered on a Likert scale (a scale of 1 – 6). A final score is given for each component and by weighting the answers and combining the individual 'P' scores following a validated algorithm, an overall **P⁶PROP®** score and profile can be reported back.

The individual profile allows a certified performance coach to make a precise analysis of the actual level of Personal Leadership Excellence, to plan and initiate a program for development and to monitor progress. This means the **P⁶PROP®** model can be used as a diagnostic tool by business champions and their organizations to assess the current status of excellence, their current potential for excellent performance and as a tool to further develop individual performance.

Applying the P⁶PROP® model

If you would like to use the P⁶PROP® model profile yourself and/or your organization with the exclusive support of Christian Marcolli or one of his certified performance coaches, please review the entry criteria as well as the bespoke coaching and support packages on the following website www.p6prop.com. The website also provides detailed information about how you can access P⁶PROP® for events, corporate courses, and presentations.

MARCOLLI
EXECUTIVE
EXCELLENCE

Marcolli Executive Excellence provides organizations with practical, inspiring and highly impactful programs for their leaders and teams. Since 1997, Marcolli Executive Excellence has maintained a long-term cooperation with a number of international companies and helped many leaders and teams to achieve outstanding performance. For more information please visit: www.marcolli.com.